In(TY)tyled Thoughts: Keep space for me

Tyicia DeLoney

Presentation by *BookLeaf Publishing*

Web: www.bookleafpub.com

E-mail: info@bookleafpub.com

ISBN: 9789357695466

First edition 2022

PREFACE

After I said

I can't sleep
It's you runnin through my mind
I can't eat
Cause it seems I'm running outta time (pounds)
I can't weep
Cause there's too much water I don't wanna
drown
I can't think
Cause it's overdue and look what's goin down
I wanna sink
You been my gem a rocks too naturale
I wanna meet
You gave me joy and that's something unfound
I wanna speak
The words so ancient I utter but there's no
sounds
And that's the thing..

Is it forever for you?

To have a plethora of names
Since birth and from beyond
From friend and mi Amor
The light of pain nothing but a button I push
over and over again to ignore
To keep from going further
Do you know limitless love?
Or are you bound to the worries
I refuse to take away what I've been birthed to
give back
I receive it all in no hurry
Cause where you stumble and walk around
I fall
Mother Earth cemented a historical call into
your essence
Never saddened when I get shoveled
leaving me grounded absorbing the puddle
Cause you let me carry you through it
And I would never ignore your ring-calls
(wrinkles)
A love like mine you felt
A crushed heart, thawed to a melt
Miss na miss kita you say to me
And here I am missing you from my car
Because tu corazon reached out and

How can I just leave you scarred?

But that's the last memory I have with you
Sucks you never vroom-vroomed to my heart
Sucks to feel less than full and fully apart
Shatters of agony and resonances of love left in
my name
Now that's art
But sharing my sufferings with you..
Let me depict the view

On a Tuesday in February

I inhaled the hate given and I exhale joy
anyways
It's semi-automatic, must be for you
cause I hesitate everything on my personal plate

I inhal'd your splattered pain, and I exhale so
many reinforcements
Never occurring to you reciprocity is my least
favorite game, but you endorsed it
Tightenin' the reigns, my corset strapped lungs,
of course you never saw me gasp
You never knew real love, so confident in the
front
The air was so thin, I couldn't help sheddin'
within what was
Or was it what it wasn't from the jump?

I inhaled your smiles for the last, and I exhale
this pure new breath
So strange I never knew I needed this redo
to glee upon death because I literally had
nothing left
For myself
Smiling because I have relish over fear
deflecting my essence

my spiritual aura fueled with generations of
ancient ancestry
It's fact, making the wrong choice again wasn't
in my reality
It was all a dream anyways
So don't forget to remember me while you sleep
A glimpse of me appealing to your days

Tall miles

It's the way your kiss lingers
How can I hide this smile?
You moved my aura, my spirit jiggled
My mind is running on your tall miles
It must be a first
I love, I am
Even when I'm tryna hide

Wednesday's Pain

I had to put on my face so many times
Like all this smiling is really gonna get me
somewhere
People like "ohh what a beautiful disguise"
I think, smile and nod
Yes just say thank you
Or don't say nothing, that's right
Mother always reminded us "if ya ain't got
nothing nice to say, don't say nothing at all"
Is there anyone else that takes words literal or to
the heart?
Cause mother knew what to say to make her rain
go away
I just sit there, watch her mouth bend
Pretending everything was okay
Then smile and wave cause it was hard for me to
sit with the pain
I never wanted you to feel the constant rain
saved amidst a sunny day

Forever Mi Villa

Benita Villa she wears jewelry on her fingers
She wears it in her sleep
She takes a lil nap and she shines on fleek
I am a Villa
Aye que chula mija
Mi reign
Pobrecita
She always blessed my soul
Por vida por vida por vida
Señorita es la mejor abuelita

Sunnyvale

If magic ain't real, then how am I here?
Why the past keep tryna take front and center
knowing its place is the rear
I wanna travel the world and yet my baggage
keep clippin my heal
And I'm not talkin bout my feet
Cause the adventure is destined for me
It's even hard to speak
Cause the speed slows then stops
Stutters and then hits repeat
It could never be with you I compete

Who am I? Am I Over?

When I get "over" something
It's like all my senses are jumpin
Like I'm overthinking
Over being
Over achieving to be
Onboard
Over stipulation
Causing stimulation
Do the rules account for the summation?
It's an oversight in need of deflation
A new way to delegate and then sum
Mentally over fun
The ways of one turn into alone
And then . .I'm over the sun
No, over the moon
Reaching for the light only stars can provide
I speak to exist, I leap over hide
I further to find . . I (eye)

A mentally.. Noted

I don't know how to be otherwise
To uplift and inspire
That's what I desire
My life fueled with combustion
Burning the midnight fire
And even if I tear myself down
I build you up, help you plant your flowers
Your garden deserves to be honored
I too have a right to the harvest
Even though I fall deep in the decline
I promise to continue to climb
I promise to move forward in time
I promise to put self first
I promise to feed your brain with star bursts
Praying it gives inches to the pain your heart
thirsts
I promise to yearn in the rememories in my mind
Just because I can tell the time doesn't mean I'm
on the clock and I promise you..
I promise you I'm always ready to take another
shot
Take a shot for me and reteach what you knew
Just forgot

Rere (riri) Song

Readjust
Realigned
Rejuvenating
Redo the edges like restoration
Restore the nation
Recalibrate your taste buds, yea
Rethink them taste buds
Reread the line
Reread the book
Reread the time
Retake the look

Speed Racer

Don't take it personal is real
Cause then YOU take on what they feel and
That can CHANGE your energy at the wheel
And YOU don't wanna be driving like that..

Cherish Tree

Stand tall like momma made you
Like grandma gave you
The strength you'll need to breakthrough
It's ancestral
What they raised
You grew
What they craved
You pursued
There's no end to the depth
No feelings
This all brand new
Take what you learn
Unlearn that too
Keep the lost gems sacred
Your most cherished parts of you

Tbh

I never dreamed of more money, more trees
Cause growin up in poverty, mom supplied my
needs
Money never ruled the world around me
But somehow the cash bought the cream
My dreams been bigger then me
Sometimes I give up knowin'
Cause in this world, fame is where they glowin'
But my shine started when I had nothing
I pray I don't switch up, get clouded by the
greed
The IG feed..

No date, any time

Here comes the season of giving and
No matter how hard I push down my feelings
They creep up with no TLC and all chillings
Depression is . .but I'm still healing

"Love" is my middle name

I feel like all I ever was is grounded
An uprooted tree firmly planted
And I just wanted to fly
Spread my wings, become enchanted
My free spirit never cemented
Cause I've been chosen
And that's ever-lasting. .
Not unknowing
To discover your innate whole
The magic bestoweth'
Take a broom and sweep up the unholy
You see only what I chose to show thee
Them pieces where always meant to fall
By the universe I am, I'll be all
I rebuild with the crumble
And dismantle your ego
Screaming with an ancestral call
I will rise above
I am more than part of the people

1:33am

I don't wanna protest
I don't want my face on a shirt
I hope after I die you still share my history and
my worth
What is an ally?
I hope you see me before I take my last breath
I know I'll forever be the reason for Earth
I hope you never forget

Man it's crazy being a woman

Man it's crazy being a woman
Sure being sexual is a thing
But no one ever really talks about the after just
in-between
The aftermath of being in them jeans
Man, it's crazy to be a woman
Having to decide in them moments
Are they who suppose to be 'worth it'
My moms always said to wait
But how do you know when it's too late
How do you stay away before your heart breaks
Man, it's crazy being a woman
If everyones playing games then which ones do I
play
Or why didn't you teach me to walk away
Oh I get it.
That would be a shame
Too embarrassing to give up embarazada
So keeping a child to place the blame is one way
Man, it's crazy being a woman
Being able to say to your kid "I'm here, I
stayed" and
In the same sentence giving them your pain and

Repeating again how 'I coulda left you like ya
daddy did in a haste'
And as you just walk away leaving me standing
in the hallway
I wonder..
Man, it's crazy being a woman
Would I feel better if I was left at a fire station
Having no one make the choice to choose me
I guess it depends on how you see it or feel
That decision is almost always still up to . .
Man, it's crazy being a woman. Foreal

A kept shower thought

The people in the past must have been greedy
Like, cause it's disgusting to want to trap minds
that move so freely
To enslave the minds of daughters and sons
Descendants of Nefertiti
Now that's a kind of blasphemy
Maybe each century is a way to start over
Except no we just had rulers upon rulers settling
the earth
Reburying the soil
How can we be in 2022 and not have much to
show for
I guess it just depends on who showed up for
Her
A little tender love and care never hurt
But It was always the first choice x'd out in dirt